THE SEVERN VALLEY RAILWA

AT

ARLEY

REVISED EDITION

BY

BARRIE GEENS

From an original painting by Sean Bolan

WILD SWAN PUBLICATIONS LTD.

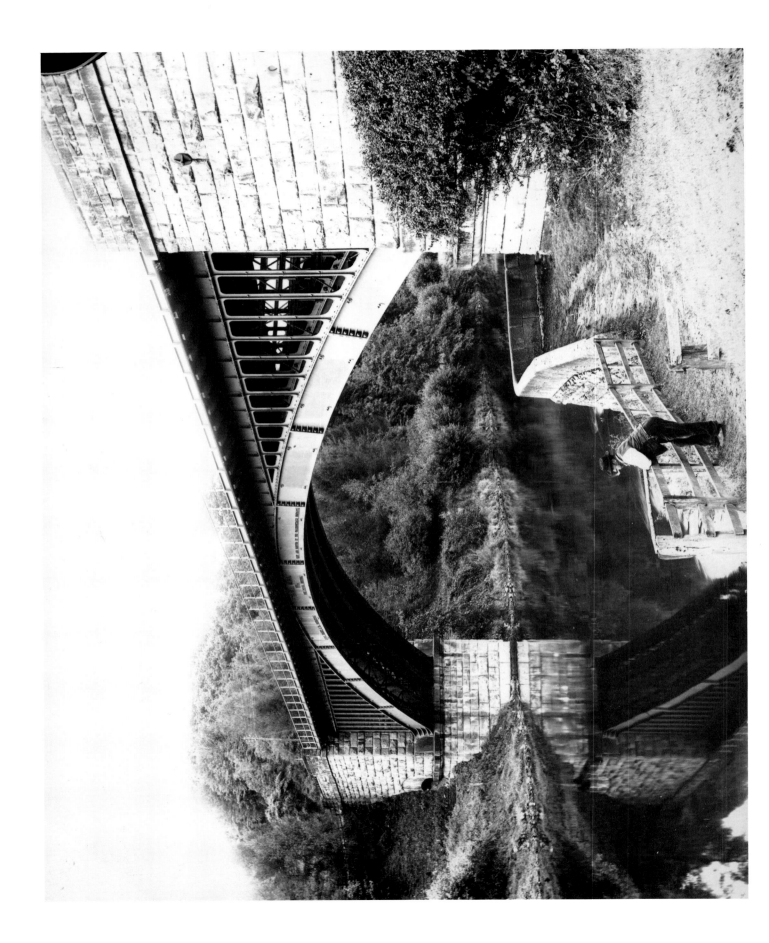

ARLEY STATION

Its Origins, Development and Characters — 1862-1963

BETWEEN 1845 and 1852 various schemes were considered for a railway linking Shrewsbury and Worcester. Interest was at its height by the summer of 1852 and within a year the Severn Valley Railway was incorporated, the Bill presented at Westminster receiving the Royal Assent on 20th August 1853.

The capital of the company for the construction of a double track main line was originally fixed at £600,000, but in 1856 this could not be raised and when the scheme was nearly abandoned it became imperative to cut costs drastically. This was achieved by agreeing that the line should be made single throughout, leaving room for a second track if traffic warranted. Plans to build bridges across the Severn at Shrewsbury, Bridgnorth and Quatford were also abandoned. Despite these troubles, the Severn Valley line was eventually leased to the Oxford, Worcester

and Wolverhampton Railway for an extended term, and in 1858 construction work eventually began with Messrs. Brassey, Peto and Betts as main contractors and John Fowler as engineer.

During its construction the *Worcester Herald* claimed that the Severn Valley line appealed to the 'antiquarian, artist and scientist', several field clubs and private naturalists visiting the cutting near Arley to view the interesting fossils and sections of rock strata. It was known as the Great Cutting and had a maximum depth of sixty feet.

Just to the south of Arley station, the Victoria Bridge carries the line from Shropshire over the Severn to Worcestershire and on to Bewdley. It was to have been one of four railway bridges over the Severn between Hartlebury and Shrewsbury but, as already mentioned, plans for the other three were abandoned. Designed to take double track, this impressive

structure, in every way the most outstanding and costly feature of the line, totalled some £8,500.

The laying of the foundation stone took place at 3 o'clock in the afternoon on Thursday, 24th November 1859. Mr. H. O. Bridgman, CE, officiated at the ceremony and received an engraved silver trowel (now displayed at the National Railway Museum at York) from Mr. Day representing the contractors. The ceremony was further assisted by Mr. Sharp, clerk of the works. Having laid the stone, Mr. Bridgman christened it with a bottle of wine and named the bridge 'Victoria Bridge' in honour of the reigning sovereign. He then addressed the friends of the company and numerous spectators, ending with 'Three cheers for the Severn Valley Railway and the Severn Bridge'.

Under the foundation stone a large bottle was buried, containing coins of the realm in current usage, and a scroll of

Opposite: *Victoria Bridge around the turn of the century.* Above: *An idyllic Edwardian study on the bank of the Severn alongside Victoria Bridge.*
BRITISH RAILWAYS and KIDDERMINSTER LIBRARY

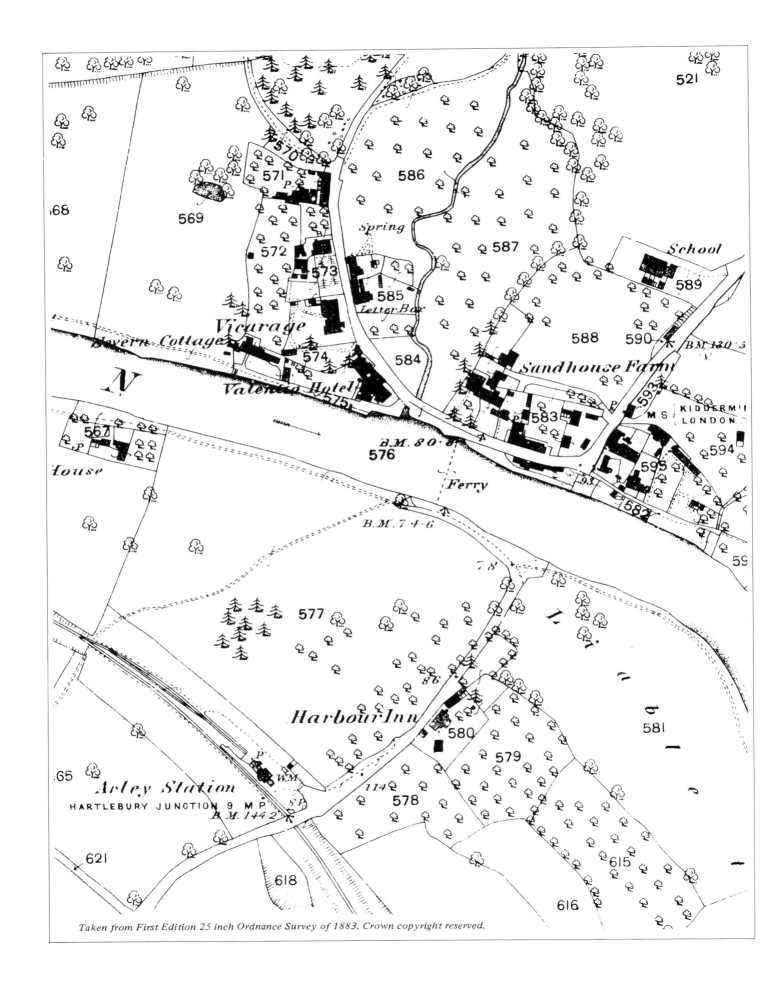

Arley Ferry.

Courtesy GEORGE BLOUNT

paper signed by the principal witnesses. At the head of the scroll was the following inscription:

The Foundation Stone of the Bridge was laid by Henry Orlando Bridgman, Esq., C.E., Resident Engineer on the 24th day of November in the Year of Our Lord One Thousand, Eight Hundred and Fifty Nine, and the twenty third year of the reign of Her Majesty Queen Victoria.

The arch of the bridge is to be constructed principally of cast iron with a 200 ft. span — and, up to the present time, will be the largest cast iron bridge in the Kingdom. (signed) John Fowler, Esq., Engineer-in-chief, London. Messrs. Brassey, Peto and Betts, Contractors, also of London.

The castings for the bridge were produced to the specifications of John Fowler at Coalbrookdale Iron Works. They were designed to bear a weight of 40 tons to the square inch. Contemporary reports state that a defective rib casting was tested to destruction under a load of 430 tons and that on a hot summer's day during construction, the arch ribs lifted 1½ inches off the scaffolding underneath, but with no visible rotation at the abutment bearings. Total span is double that of the first iron bridge at Ironbridge (opened 1779), the central or river arch being 200 ft. Height from spring to crown of the central arch is 20 ft. Two 30 ft

land arches, to take flood water, were built, one on either side of the central arch.

After the ceremony invited guests adjourned to a celebration dinner held at the Lion Hotel, Worcester Street, Kidderminster, catering and entertainment being supervised by the landlord, Mr. M. Rheades. The chairman of the dinner was Mr. Field, representing the contractors, supported by Mr. Day as vice-chairman. Those present included the mayors of Bewdley and Kidderminster, directors of the company and leading shareholders.

While the celebrities enjoyed their banquet, a party of about a hundred workmen employed on the Victoria Bridge site were entertained in 'traditional English style' at the Harbour Inn.

Following heavy rain in the spring and early summer of 1860, the cutting near Victoria Bridge suffered a 25 ft slip which involved considerable remedial work but on Friday, 10th May 1861, the last girder to form the river arch of the bridge was fixed into place. Work on the land arches and approaches to the bridge were finished some six weeks later.

On 1st November 1860 the West Midland Railway had leased the Severn Valley line from the OW & W Railway on a 999 year lease. There then followed a chapter of accidents which delayed the

opening of the line which was set for early 1861. The first incident was the collapse of the tunnel entrance at Bridgnorth, which was blocked to a depth of 50 ft by a mass of rubble and tree trunks and took a considerable time to clear. On 9th January 1861 a ganger, Jessie Bishop, was killed by an explosion while employed in cutting Mount Pleasant Tunnel midway between Stourport and Bewdley. He appears to have been in charge of blasting operations and, caught within the danger area at the time of the explosion, was struck by a shower of broken rock.

The line was finally opened on 31st January 1862, a special train leaving Shrub Hill station, Worcester, for the opening run to Shrewsbury at 11.30 a.m., stopping at various stations and returning to Worcester after an evening celebration at Bridgnorth.

An interesting minute from the Severn Valley Railway Co. board meeting on 26th May 1853 records 'It was resolved that an agreement be entered into with Mr. Robert Woodward of Arley Castle to the effect that the ordinary trains of the Company shall stop at the Arley Station to take up Mr. Woodward, wife and children upon half an hour's previous notice being given to the Station Master at Arley.' However, it is not clear whether

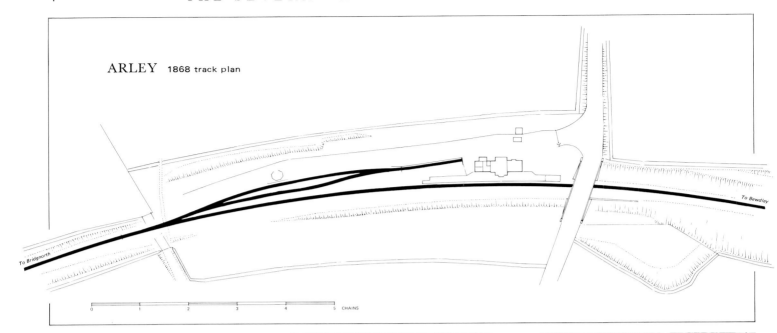

ARLEY 1868 track plan

To Bridgnorth

To Bewdley

0   1   2   3   4   5 CHAINS

this was enforced by the time the line was opened and if so for how long the practice continued.

The West Midland Railway Company, which supplied locomotives and rolling stock, was dissolved in 1863, its rights and obligations being vested in the Great Western Railway, the Severn Valley Railway Company being amalgamated with the Great Western Railway under the GWR Act of 1st July 1872.

The new owners improved the line by providing a more direct and convenient link between the Birmingham area and points north of Bewdley. This was achieved by the construction of a loop line linking Bewdley with Kidderminster which opened on 1st June 1878. Despite this link, the line was never to become a highly profitable concern, its main function in latter years being to serve the pits of the Severn Valley Coalfield. It was never more than a country branch except during the two world wars when it was used as a bypass route for the industrial West Midlands.

Arley station was originally confined to a single short platform on the northern or 'up' side of the running line, with, by the time of the first Ordnance Survey c.1880, a compact goods yard and weigh-bridge behind the platform. The brick-built station building/dwelling offered the public a waiting room and booking office and a gentlemen's lavatory, but no such facilities for ladies. The rest of the structure provided the station master and his family with a parlour, kitchen, pantry, W.C., outside scullery and two upstairs bedrooms.

The station was upgraded in 1883 when a crossing loop and second or

Home Farm, Upper Arley.   Courtesy GEORGE BLOUNT

'down' platform and shelter were added. The new arrangements involved reconnecting the goods siding to the new 'down' running line to avoid a now unnecessary facing connection, the west end of the sidings themselves being slewed to connect. The new layout was fully signalled and controlled from a new signal box which, situated in the centre of the layout for mechanical reasons and on the outside of the curve for sighting purposes, was subsequently situated in the goods yard behind the sidings. From official plans of the alterations it seems likely that the station building was also enlarged

at this time to provide a ladies waiting room and lavatory. The eastern extension was carefully matched to the original and the modest glazed canopy over the platform elevation, which, again according to drawings already existed, was also extended. Later, in 1901, a third bedroom was also added to the upper storey above the pantry at the western end.

The last major work at Arley was carried out in 1907 when the crossing loop was lengthened and both platforms extended in a westerly direction together with a corresponding move of the down

G.W.R.

ARLEY.

Distant 9 Miles 0 Chains from Junction of the Severn Valley R.º with Worcester & Wolverhampton R.º

SCALE 66 FEET TO ONE INCH

LEVEL

1 IN 100

500 Yds

Official GWR track plan showing 1883 alterations.

G.W.R — ARLEY STATION

PROPOSED ALTERATIONS AND ADDITIONS

SCALE OF [10 ... Feet 6 ... 0 ... 5 ... 10 ... 15 ... 20 ... 25 ... 30 ... 35 ... 40 ... 45] FEET

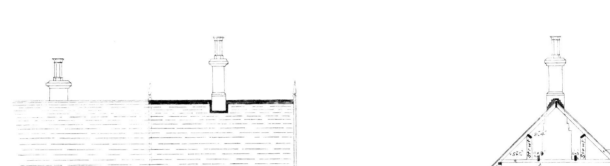

— ELEVATION TOWARDS RAILS —

RAILS

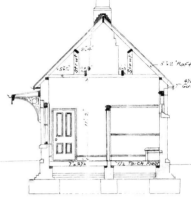

— SECTION AT A B —

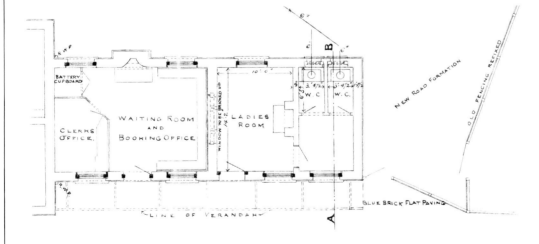

These alterations and additions, which included provision of a Ladies waiting room with WC, were completed in 1892 for a cost of £240.

— GROUND PLAN —

SCALE — 2 mm to 1 foot

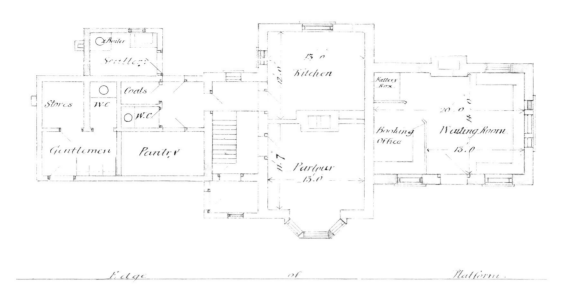

Boiler
Scullery
Coals
Stores
W.C.
W.C.
Gentlemen
Pantry

13.0
Kitchen
12.0

Battery Box
Booking Office
Waiting Room
20.0
14.0
13.0

11.7
Parlour
13.0

Edge   of   Platform.

Arley

Proposed Bedroom for Station Master's House

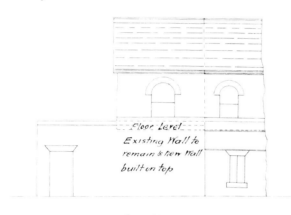

Floor Level
Existing Wall to
remain & new Wall
built on top

The extra bedroom shown here was added in
1901 at a cost of £65.

Elevation

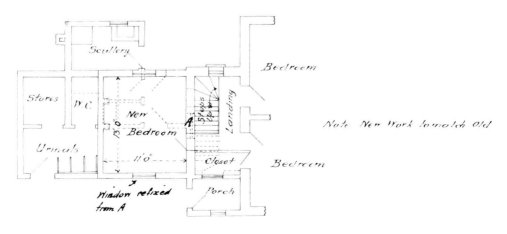

Scullery
Bedroom
Stores
W.C.
New
Bedroom
13.0
Landing
A
5 steps
Note New Work to match Old
Urinals
11'0"
Closet
Bedroom
Window relixed
from A
Porch

Plan of First Floor

Taken from three official plans

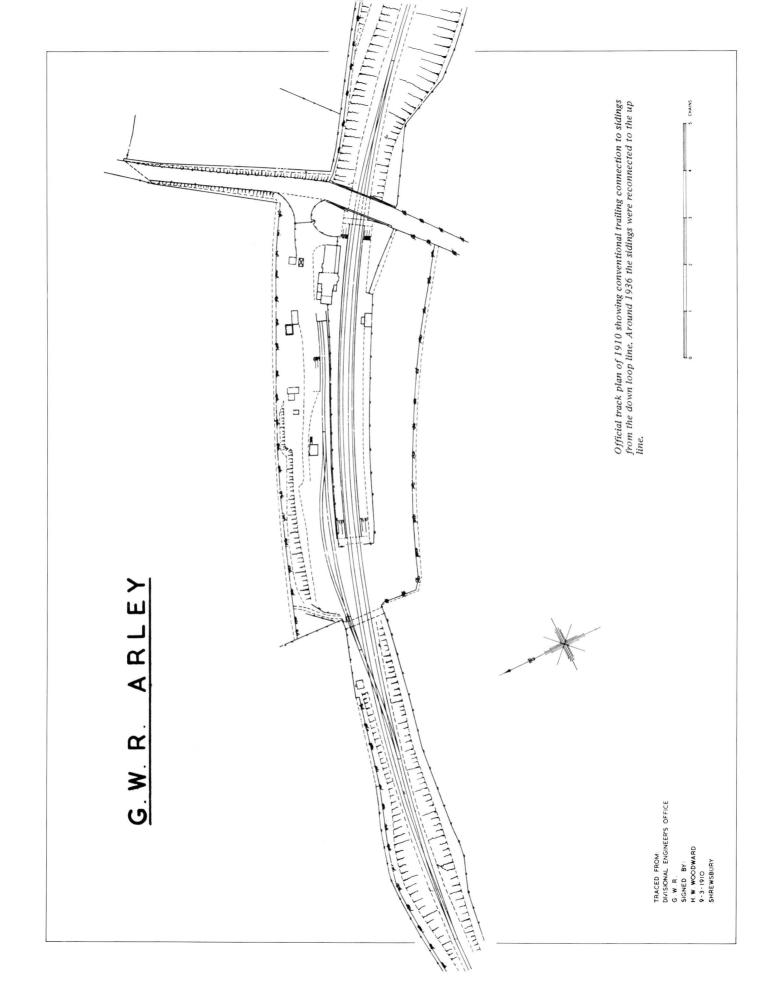

G.W.R. ARLEY

Official track plan of 1910 showing conventional trailing connection to sidings from the down loop line. Around 1936 the sidings were reconnected to the up line.

TRACED FROM:
DIVISIONAL ENGINEER'S OFFICE
G. W. R.
SIGNED BY:
H. W. WOODWARD
9-3-1910
SHREWSBURY

5 CHAINS
0   1   2   3   4

A general view and enlarged section of the same print of the station buildings c.1902, showing the brand new station master's bedroom and the 'up' platform fence in its original position, level with the front of the gents' toilet wall. Note track with inside keys and tall down home and up starting signals. The porter/signalman is also holding the Arley to Highley staff.

Collection M. F. YARWOOD

This picture, taken c.1905 before the platforms were extended, clearly shows the new brickwork on the bedroom extension.

starting and up home signals. The improvements again involved the disturbance of the goods sidings which, reconnected further west to allow for the extension of the 'up' platform, were lengthened slightly and completely re-aligned and/or probably relaid. These improvements were accompanied by a new end loading bank, the provision of a corrugated iron goods lock-up alongside the yard, the movement of a fence to allow metalling 20 ft wide alongside the rearmost loop siding, and consequent refixing of the adjacent accommodation crossing gate, what appears to have been a new oil hut near the signal box, a platelayers hut at the west end of the layout, and the replacement of the weighbridge and office, although it is just possible the latter may have been replaced in 1883. A new approach path was also made between the road bridge and the 'down' platform.

The following are some interesting notes taken from the Arley station book of working instructions, 1895:

'The cash books at this station are closed at 7.40 p.m. The cash is made up at 7.40 p.m. and remitted daily in the following manner in accordance with the instructions of the Chief Cashier. viz. First train in the morning following to Worcester.

Station Inspector's Duties

1. To take charge of the passenger Station and Goods Yard and to keep a general supervision over the shunting &c.
2. **Passenger Trains**
   To see that the shunting operations are carefully and properly performed and that the trains, if starting from a station, are properly equipped and that the connections in the time-table are maintained so far as this station is concerned.
3. **Goods Trains**
   To see to the working of goods trains and to the prompt dispatch of traffic &c.
4. **General Duties**
   To keep proper supervision over the station staff and examine and sign the Train Book.
5. To visit the station occasionally when off duty at irregular periods.
6. To see that the closets and urinals are flushed with water and station premises kept clean and tidy.
7. To see that the staff perform their duties satisfactorily and the scale of hours adhered to.
8. To see that the stationery and stores are economically used.
9. To see that the accounts at this station are rendered in due time and all correspondence properly answered.
10. To make up and remit cash at appointed time as per instructions.
11. To pay the wages cash immediately after receipt from cashier.
12. To meet all trains with the exception of alternate Sundays and when off duty when trains are met by porter.
13. **Accidents**
    In case of accidents where assistance is required a telegram must be sent to Mr. Giles, Worcester (Loco Dept.) informing him of the nature of the accident and likewise one to Mr. Allen, London, and Roberts, Worcester, and a general detail given in letter to Mr. Roberts.
14. To report all damage to stock to Superintendent, Worcester.
15. To see that a list of fogmen is kept in the signal box and office.
16. To see that time books and bills are distributed and a signature obtained.
17. To see that the staff are supplied with copies of the Service Book.
18. To see that the staff carry out the instructions contained in the book of Rules and Regulations, the Block Telegraph Instructions and Service Book regulations at this station.
19. Responsible for working electric train staff between Arley and Highley and Arley and Bewdley North box and arrange for the safe working of the traffic in general.

To come on duty alternate Sundays half an hour before the trains are due each way

The platform extensions were well under way when this picture was taken in August 1907. The down home signal shown in the top picture of page 9 had been removed, possibly in connection with alterations at this end. The signals at both ends were repositioned at this time and sited further from the station. The platform fence near to the gentlemen's lavatory had also been set further back. DAVID POSTLE

This picture, taken during the summer of 1907, shows the newly finished platform extension but with the 'up' side not yet in use. The down starting and up home signals are still in their pre-extension positions. AUTHOR'S COLLECTION

A similar view c.1908 with the platform and fence now finished and new platform lamps. A smaller down starting signal has been erected further away from the station and the up home is now out of sight. An Armstrong goods on a freight is featured awaiting the arrival of an 'up' passenger.

AUTHOR'S COLLECTION

and take charge of the whole work of the station.

Signal Porter's Duties

1. The signal box at this station is in charge of the porters and all the points and levers working from the same. All block and single needle instruments to be attended to by them. The times of the signalling of trains to be duly entered in the book set apart for that purpose. Responsible for working electric train staff between Arley and Highley and Arley and Bewdley North box when Station Inspector is off duty.

2. To light fires in the Waiting Rooms during winter when required and to clean and light all signal and platform lamps and extinguish and bring lamps to the lamp room after the last train has passed.

3. To keep the tanks well filled with water for flushing the closets and urinals and to cleanse the same.

4. To assist in shunting operations and to help to load and unload the goods traffic.

5. To label all luggage belonging to passengers and assist with the traffic on the platform generally.

6. To take down all old time bills when an alteration takes place in the train service of the Company.

7. To forward and receive messages at this station and also all others on the service of the Company.

8. To sweep and clean the platforms and Waiting Rooms.

9. To clean all cattle wagons, horse boxes &c and to do all other outside work.

   To come on duty alternate Sundays half an hour before the trains are due each way and take charge of the whole work of the station.

Special Instructions and Special Arrangements

Weighing Machines
The small one in the Waiting Room and the Cart weighbridge to be kept in order by H. Pooley & Son.

Persons allowed a monthly account
R. Woodward, Esq., Arley Castle.
Rev. C. J. Wilding, Arley Vicarage.
Mr. G. Fletcher, Valentia Arms Hotel, Arley.

Petty Cash – £1 allowed for station purposes.

Wages Cash
Received 3.33 p.m. train Thursday and paid immediately after receipt.

Staff Working
The Severn Valley line between these points is worked on the electric staff and block telegraph system which was brought into use October 22nd, 1893.

Section   Bewdley (T & B Jnc.) and Arley
               Arley and Highley

The person authorised to exchange the staff at this station is as under

   The signalman – on duty at all times.

Station Master's hours of duty
Batchelor, G.   From 7.20 a.m. to 7.20 p.m.
                 Dinner from 1.0 - 2.0
                 Tea from 4.0 - 5.0

The station master, Mr. Batchelor, and children by his prize-winning gardens c.1905.

BRITISH RAILWAYS

Uniform Staff hours of duty
Barnett, B.   From 6.45 a.m. to 6.45 p.m.
(Sig./Porter)   Dinner from 11.0 to 12.0
                 Tea from 4.0 - 4.30

Grubb, A.   From 10.15 a.m. to 10.15 p.m.
(Sig./Porter)   Dinner from 2.0 to 3.0
                 Tea from 5.30 to 6.00

The above change duties alternate weeks.

Special rights or privileges possessed by the public
N. Perrins is permitted to walk the line between Arley Station and Severn Bridge.

In true Great Western tradition the station gardens at Arley were tended with much loving pride, particularly during the early years of the century when Mr. Batchelor, the station master, was well known for the upkeep which merited the following paragraph in the *Great Western Magazine*:

'Much satisfaction was evinced in Upper Arley at the announcement that the Company had awarded the Station Master, Mr. Batchelor, the special prize for 1909 for the best kept station garden in the division. Mr. Batchelor was also awarded special prizes in 1903, 1904 and 1905. Being then barred from the special prize he was awarded firsts in 1906, 1907 and 1908 so that for the past seven years he had won the highest prizes possible for which he was eligible. His efforts to make the station attractive have been very successful, and it is said to be his ambition to have the prettiest station on the Great Western System.'

The station was at its busiest in the 1920s when day trippers used to flock down the station bank towards the river in droves. According to the older generation in the village, the trains always ran to time, with additional services on Sundays. Some 3rd class return fares during the 1930s were – Arley to Highley 10d. Arley to Kidderminster 1/2d. and a Wednesday ticket to Worcester was 2/4d.

The original signal box at Arley Station, supplied by McKenzie and Holland, was completed in 1883 along with Highley and Hampton Loade. It was

'927' class 0—6—0 No. 946 on a Kidderminster-Shrewsbury goods leaving Arley on 11th June 1915.

'439' class 2—4—0 No. 441 leaving Arley on 11th June 1915, hauling a 6-coach rake of close-coupled four-wheelers in the lake livery. The bogie vehicle at the rear, fitted with a destination board, was probably a through slip coach working from Kidderminster or Hartlebury.

Collection H. W. BURMAN

fitted with the contractor's C and S frame with 5 inch centres and 14 levers. In 1923 the GWR rated Arley as a class 5 box with 40 marks per hour as against 46 of Highley and 62 of Kinlet. A class 5 signalman at that time earned 50/- per week. The GWR converted the locking to vertical tappet 5 bar in 1936, almost certainly in connection with the siding alterations.

Today the journey between Arley and Highley has little to distract passengers savouring the lush scenery, but in the days prior to the Second World War it was all very different. Two miles to the north of Arley lay Kinlet and Billingsley colliery sidings, where trucks of coal were brought down from both Kinlet and Billingsley collieries by the Highley Mining Company's own steam locomotives.

Kinlet and Billingsley signal box, controlling the sidings, was also a block post, the sections Arley to Kinlet and Billingsley being worked with electric train staff, picking up and setting down apparatus being used by trains not requiring to call when the box was switched in. After the day's work was completed it was switched out and all the signals, including the distant signals, were placed in the 'off' position, the section then becoming Arley to Highley and being worked with

A Kidderminster to Bridgnorth train north of Arley station, hauled by a 'Metro' tank 2—4—0 on 11th June 1915.

Collection H. W. BURMAN

An Armstrong goods with a Kidderminster-Bridgnorth goods north of Arley on 11th June 1915.   Collection H. W. BURMAN

'2201' class No. 2209 heading a Shrewsbury to Kidderminster train towards Arley, having just passed the up distant signal, on 11th June 1915.
Collection H. W. BURMAN

An unidentified 0—4—2T heading towards Arley, passing the up distant signal. The Kinlet down distant signal can just be seen above the rear of the loco.
Collection H. W. BURMAN

A south-bound coal train, hauled by an 0—6—0 Dean goods, leaving Kinlet and Billingsley sidings on 11th June 1915. Kinlet signal box and signals can be seen in the distance on the original print. Collection H. W. BURMAN

'3521' class 4—4—0 No. 3557 crossing an auto-train at Arley on 7th September 1932. Timetable research suggests this was probably the 5.04 p.m. weekday train to Shrewsbury on the 4.30 p.m. ex Hartlebury. No. 3557 was one of a class of forty rebuilt in 1899-1902 from 0—4—4Ts and broad gauge convertibles (0—4—2T) in 1890/1. It was rebuilt in November 1899 and is shown here fitted with what the RCTS classify as a 'B4 domed boiler'. It was one of four of the class that were allocated to Kidderminster for working the Tenbury branch, Severn Valley and trains to Birmingham. The others, Nos. 3535, 3555 and 3529, were withdrawn from Kidderminster in December 1928, September 1929 and April 1931 respectively. No. 3557 was the last survivor of the class, not being withdrawn from Kidderminster until May 1934.

SELWYN PEARCE-HIGGINS, CTY. NATIONAL RAILWAY MUSEUM

the electric train tablet, the only one on the branch.

Following the closure of Billingsley pit in 1921 and Kinlet in 1935, the signal box was eventually dismantled on Sunday, 20th June 1943, when it was replaced by a ground frame at each end unlocked with the electric train token for the Arley to Highley section.

During and prior to the Second World War, the sidings were used by Messrs. Wagon Repairs Ltd., of Gloucester, for repairing private owner coal wagons, most of them being 10 or 12 tons carrying capacity from the power station at Stourport. Empty wagons for repair were worked forward and berthed at Arley station and picked up on Tuesdays and Fridays by the 12 o'clock coal train, Kidderminster to Alveley sidings. The Severn Valley branch was a very important link with the war effort, remaining open 24 hours a day for long periods to relieve the heavily congested main lines.

Joe Hill was the last residential station master at Arley until he transferred to Fernhill Heath in the early 1930s. The porter/signalmen under him were Fred Jones and Fred Leek. After Joe's departure Arley was put under the supervision of Bewdley and the house was occupied by Fred Jones.

Born in 1896, and step-son of Mr. Stanley who was station master at Hampton Loade, Fred, who served over 50 years on the GWR and BR, had lived in one of the cottages on the other side of the river prior to marrying and moving to the station. His wife Diane, who had worked at Arley Castle when they were first married, was trained at Worcester and became porter/signalman. During the war years when the station was manned 'round the clock', they each worked alternate 12 hour shifts. At this time additional help was provided by their daughter, Chris, and later their son, David, who joined the railway as a fireman and regularly worked the branch. In fact he exchanged tokens with his mother for the last time on the final passenger train to run over the line on 7th September 1963. Changing the token was a fairly straightforward operation if the train was stopping, whereas running straight through on a goods train presented a tense situation for many young firemen. It meant leaning over the side of a rocking, swaying cab, releasing their token and catching the fresh one at the exact moment they passed the signalman. Catch the token at the wrong angle and they would suffer a badly bruised hand or a broken finger, as one fireman did.

Fred was quite a character and used to worry some of the train crews by delaying until the last possible moment his arrival on the barrow crossing with the token. As one fireman recalled, on approaching Arley they would give a blast on the whistle to remind him they were not far away. The station would come into sight but often no sign of Fred. Another blast on the whistle and, as the train was rapidly approaching the station, Fred appeared from the station buildings, and stopped to look up at the sky to consider the weather! Whatever the weather Fred's attire was always the same, crumpled cap, khaki army shirt, railway trousers held in position by either a leather belt or an old tie, no socks and either plimsolls or slippers, depending on whether he had been gardening or reading the paper! "He's coming, but I don't reckon he'll make it", said the fireman. Fred slowly ambled along the wet and deserted platform, stopped, bent down to pick up a piece of paper, studied it and resumed his slow pace towards the end of the platform. The fireman anxiously leant over the side of the cab, preparing to exchange tokens. With the rain like a thousand icy sharp needles against the fireman's hands and face, screwing up his eyes against the rain, he saw Fred slowly ambling down the platform slope just as they prepared to pass under the road bridge. When the tokens were exchanged, Fred's grizzled, rain-soaked face looked up to the fireman. "Nice now" he said as the train rushed by and then he ambled back up the platform at the same steady pace towards the station buildings. Fred had the timing to a fine art and in all his years he was rarely known to miss.

Fred was also a St. John Ambulance man and villagers would always send for him before anyone else. He was also noted for his attire; he hardly ever wore socks; in fact even when he went to London for a day during his holidays he

A young Fred Jones with his step-mother, Mrs. Stanley, c.1932.

GLADYS BILLINGHAM

This picture shows '517' class No. 1440 which, having just crossed 3557 (see picture on page 18) was awaiting the 'right away' at Arley on 7th September 1932. This is believed to have been the 5.08 p.m. auto-train to Kidderminster, 4.37 p.m. ex Bridgnorth. The 0–4–2T loco was built in December 1877 and fitted for auto working in January 1925, having been provided with an enclosed cab the previous year. From 1929 onwards it worked autos around the Kidderminster triangle and up the Severn Valley together with main line auto-trains between Kidderminster and Worcester, for which it was fitted for Automatic Train Control (ATC) at some time between June 1930 and September 1931. Following the arrival of Collett 0–4–2T No. 4816, new to Kidderminster in May 1933, No. 1440 spent some time on loan to Worcester before ending up at Weymouth where it was withdrawn in September 1935. Coach No. 39 was a conversion from steam railmotor No. 98. It was 63ft 6in long and had 64 seats. The coach was withdrawn (probably from Kidderminster) in June 1933.

SELWYN PEARCE-HIGGINS, CTY. NATIONAL RAILWAY MUSEUM

wore his white pumps and no socks! He regularly frequented the 'Harbour' when Mrs. Hall was licensee and she recalled that he was a very good cider customer. He used to help himself from the barrel, which was just at the top of the cellar and nearly always sat on a bench in the passage. Some days (having had one or two) Fred would suddenly say "Cheerio, I can hear a ghost train coming", and sure enough the train would often be whistling in the cutting. Cider and chewing twist were two of Fred's loves and in all the years she knew him Mrs. Hall said she never heard him swear and also never heard anyone speak ill of him. She also recalls how her children remember Fred holding the 8 o'clock morning train for them while they ran up the bank with their toast in their hands. They went to school at Bridgnorth.

Mrs. Hall was licensee at the 'Harbour' from August 1931 to 1961. Her husband was a signalman at Highley in 1919 and at Cressage previous to this. She remembered that very occasionally he would oversleep. He had to be at Highley at 5 o'clock in the morning to signal the first train in. If there was a good driver and fireman he would put his bike on the engine and hop in, get off at the distant signal, run along and all was well; otherwise when he was very late he would get a caution. Mr. Hall left the railway in 1945 and died in July 1972.

Mrs. Hall recollects that another very regular customer at the 'Harbour' was George Evans, or 'Bristler' as he was known, who was a ganger on the railway. He liked his beer and his usual seat was just inside the tap room while he joined in conversation with Fred Jones.

A story was once told in the 'Harbour' of a Birmingham camper whose knowledge of natural history was not all it should be. Famous for its nightingales which used to keep folk awake at night and also plentifully supplied with crickets, our Brummie turned up one morning claiming that he had 'caught one o' them nightingales'. Opening up his fist, he released a cricket!

The 'Harbour' was popular with many railwaymen, particularly being so close to Arley station. When he was a boy during the war years, Peter Wardle's father worked in Liverpool and was only able to join him for holidays. One of the events of his Christmas to which he and his brother looked forward, was meeting him from his train at Bewdley. As he recalls:

'The last train used to leave Shrewsbury at nine p.m. and was due at Bewdley at 10.30. Accordingly one Christmas Eve my brother and I walked down from the Forest to meet the train.

'Usually it was late. Sometimes we allowed ourselves the rare luxury of a taxi, but more

The Harbour Inn. AUTHOR

often it meant struggling the four miles home on foot, laden with bags and packages — and on one occasion with a goose that one of my father's more influential friends had given him.

'On this occasion the train was very late, and the station master invited us into his ticket office to wait there. This was a real treat! The

Mrs. Jones posed for her official GWR photograph, c.1940. GLADYS BILLINGHAM

room was small, crowded with paraphernalia and very snug. There was a roaring coal fire burning in the grate, and we were given mugs of strong, sweet tea. The station master, fat and jovial, chatted and joked pleasantly with us. Every now and then a bell would clang and he would talk into an old-fashioned telephone and ascertain the latest whereabouts of the train.

'As usual she was running late; but at long last tidings reached us "'ers left 'ighley." Not long to wait now. However, there then followed a profound silence. Ten, twenty, thirty — even forty minutes passed, and no news. Frantic calls to Arley remained unanswered. No train. Still no train.

'Eventually after more bellows down the blower, the station master announced with relief that she'd left Arley, and soon the 'Christmas Express' chuffed its way over the viaduct, round the corner and into the station.

'Why was she so late? My father soon gave us the explanation. The train had arrived at Arley with about twenty passengers on board, whereupon the driver had hopped down onto the platform and called out, "Come on, lads, how about a quick one at the 'Harbour'?". So to a man, crew and passengers had trooped down the hill and enjoyed a celebratory Christmas Eve drink at the Harbour Inn. Later, suitably refreshed, they had staggered back up the hill and resumed their journey.

'Such spontaneous manifestations of conviviality are hardly to be found on our modern British Railways!'

Arley was designated station number 34 from the Great Western period through BR days to closure, this number being shown on the various records that have survived. In the *GWR Register of Season Tickets* the first entry was 1st July, 1913,

The Jones children at the back of the station house c.1938, Christine, Gladys, Gordon and David.
The lower view features the red brick weighbridge office.   GLADYS BILLINGHAM

The list varied with sheep from Knighton to portable buildings from South Lambeth. On 12th July 1944 the following wagons arrived from Glasgow with government stores for the US Army — NE Open 89847, PO 1833, LMS 120373, SR 8197 and NE 201642.

An interesting item logged on 17th April 1938 was the arrival earlier that week of Camping Coach No. 9947 from Swindon. The first users of this vehicle were the Speight family of Sutton Coldfield who arrived on Easter Saturday, 16th April 1938. Their journey began by 'Midland Red' bus to Bull Street, Birmingham, followed by a short walk which took them to Snow Hill station where they caught the train to Kidderminster. John Speight described the remaining journey as follows: 'Kidderminster to Bewdley by tramlike one-coach shuttle service then local stopping train to Arley, ensuring that one had got into the Bridgnorth train not the Tenbury and Wooferton which started off in the same direction but turned off left at the junction about a mile to the north.'

In 1938 Hampton Loade and Arley both had camping coaches berthed in the sidings but with the outbreak of war, the coach at Arley was discontinued. According to the GWR *Camp Coaches for Happy Holidays* booklet for 1938, the coach at Arley was a type 'A' with 6 berths.

In 1938 it cost £3.00 per week to rent and a minimum of four monthly return rail tickets had to be purchased. A seven day season ticket for dogs and bicycles accompanying passengers could be bought — 5s 3d for bicycles and 2s 8d for dogs. A third class monthly return to Arley from Birmingham Snow Hill was 4s 9d, from Worcester 3s 8d and from Paddington 22s 10d.

The booklet described the site as follows:

'The approach to Arley is very picturesque — whether through the countryside of rich pasturelands and charming woods, or by the broad slow-moving Severn. Arley has the rare beauty and peace of a village 'off the beaten track' and is one of the most delightful holiday resorts in the Midlands. There are many charming walks in the surrounding countryside, and towns and villages of historic interest are within easy reach, whilst the Severn ensures the pleasures of bathing, boating and fishing. A good service of trains is available to Bewdley and Bridgnorth which are approximately 4 and 9 miles distant respectively.'

Details of camping coach No. 9947 were as follows:

Built 10th August, 1901, as No. 949 on Lot 978 by GWR and cost £428.
Diagram T36 to T37 March 1932 (when projections removed).
Length 31' 0¾". Width 8' 0¾". Height 7' 2".
Underframe iron.

for Mr. E. Doolittle of Eymore, Bewdley — between Arley and Kidderminster — valid until 30th September, 3rd class for £1 13s 0d. A regular entry was for R. Woodward of Arley Castle to travel from Arley to Paddington. A first class ticket, 3 months to 17th July 1918, cost £19 14s 6d. The last entries during 1959 were all for the Worcester Education Authority for groups of school children travelling from Arley to Bewdley. Three months ending 22nd December 1959 — 3rd class cost £2 6s 5d each child. Each child was named individually. In 1903 the passenger tickets issued at Arley numbered 17,295. By 1932, however, they had dropped to 8,366, rising again to 10,723 in 1937. The number of parcels handled also dropped from 3,219 in 1913 to 1,255 in 1937. Goods train traffic also followed a downward trend with 1,828 tons handled in 1923 and only 46 tons in 1937.

The *Ticket Requisition Book for Arley Station* of 1913 shows that on 16th May fifty 'Severn Steam Boat Company' tickets were requisitioned, Arley to Holte Fleet, the journey being by rail to Stourport, thence by steamer to Holte Fleet and back. Fifty of these tickets were also ordered for the journey to Worcester and back.

The most interesting book in my possession is the *GWR Wagons and Sheets Received Book*. The first entry in this book is on 5th January 1937, when GW Wagon No. 84075 (a Macaw B) arrived from Hatton with rails, later dispatched to Bridgnorth on 9th January 1937.

The list of items received was endless, e.g., chairs from Ironbridge, coal from Norton Junction LMS Railway, cattle feed from Tewkesbury, ashes from Wrexham, an LNER wagon of stone from Barmouth (!) and an SR wagon of coal from Huntington, Stafford.

This was the scene that greeted the Speight family of Sutton Coldfield when they arrived for their one week camp coach holiday at Arley on Easter Saturday, 16th April 1938. The camp coach can be seen in the distance at the top of the yard.   THE SPEIGHT FAMILY

Compartments 3 — 3rd class. 1 — luggage.
4 wheels 3' 6" diameter, 19' 0" wheel base.
Weight 11 ton 2 cwt. in January 1903, and 10 ton 17 cwt. in April 1936.
Built with gas but altered to incandescent gas in February 1917.
Cast iron radiators and regulators fitted March 1922.
Ran the 5.39 Kidderminster-Ludlow train (and branded as such) August 1901. Projections removed in April 1936.
Condemned 11th December 1937.
Converted to Camping Coach No. 9947 early in 1938.
Fitted with 1 kitchen, 1 living, 1 bedroom with 2 beds and 1 bedroom with 4 beds.
To traffic 9th April 1938, arriving at Arley one week later.
It appears that the coach resided at Arley for one year only according to the official GWR camp coach lists dating from 1934-1939 (inc.).
It is recorded lifted in September 1950.
Painted red-brown in May 1945. No condemned date.
It was later discovered in the South Wales re-signalling train, being in use at Newport, Cardiff and finally Port Talbot where it was condemned in 1966. It was also considered for preservation at one time.

When the railways were nationalized in 1948 the Severn Valley line became part of the Western Region of British Railways. Faced with the diminishing traffic, the new authorities soon proved the line to be uneconomic. From 1st January 1963,

On arrival, the Speight family explored the coach, its facilities and surroundings. Being the first people to use the coach at Arley, the family were greeted by a strong smell of fresh paint, and all equipment was apparently new and impeccably clean. There was no sanitation but they were issued with a key for the station lavatories. Chamber pots were provided for overnight and the slops bucket was emptied down the WC pan at the station next morning, as was the waste from the sink. The drinking water can was filled at the station standpipe and cooking was by Valor-type oil stove. Lighting was by paraffin lamp topped up from a can at the station. The children slept in curtained two-tier bunks at one end, and parents in single beds at the opposite end. The facilities are recalled as very roomy with plenty of headroom and reassuringly solid-seeming in contrast to the unsteady, lightweight feel of an orthodox caravan. There was a sense of seclusion with no inquisitive callers. The weekly provisions were purchased in the village.
THE SPEIGHT FAMILY

The camp coach was attractively sited with a fine view (between trees) of the village on the other side of the river and the castle turrets on the skyline.

THE SPEIGHT FAMILY

NOTE.—

Each of the 4 Berth Cabins is fitted with a movable bed which can, if desired, be transferred to the Cabin fitted with 2 Berths.

A ... Draining Board.   D ... Stove, with Oven.
B ... Sink.   E ... Cupboard.
C ... Table.   F ... Wardrobe.
    G ... Cloakroom, with Wash Basin.

Type "A"—6 Berths.

SEVERN VALLEY

ARLEY (Type "A").

The approach to Arley is very picturesque whether through the countryside of rich pasture lands and charming woods, or by the broad slow-moving Severn.

Arley has the rare beauty and peace of a village "off the beaten track" and is one of the most delightful holiday resorts in the Midlands. There are many charming walks in the surrounding countryside, and towns and villages of historic interest are within easy reach, whilst the river ensures the pleasure of bathing, boating and fishing. A good service of trains is available at Bewdley and Bridgnorth, which are approximately 4 and 9 miles distant respectively.

HAMPTON LOADE (Type "A").

Hampton Loade is a picturesque hamlet situated four miles south of Bridgnorth, in a part of the Severn Valley, famed for its beauty. It is an ideal centre for rambles, and the River Severn, which adjoins the coach, is available for fishing. Boats may be hired from Bridgnorth. A convenient service of trains is available from Bridgnorth where boating can be enjoyed.

GWR
CAMP COACH HOLIDAYS
CAMPING IN COMFORT AT SELECTED BEAUTY SPOTS
NOVEL AND INEXPENSIVE

Courtesy Birmingham Public Libraries

This view shows a train headed by a Dean Goods simmering gently on the down line and a line of empty private owner coal wagons on the siding behind the platform. These were destined either for the collieries around Highley or awaiting repair by Messrs. Wagon Repairs Ltd., of Gloucester. The camp coach just features behind — no health and safety rules in those days!
THE SPEIGHT FAMILY

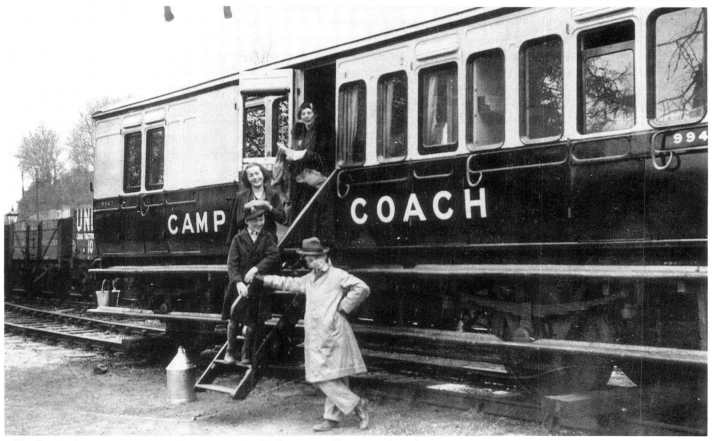

The Speight family on the steps of the camp coach with John, aged 15, wearing father's trilby, his brother Richard, aged 11, in school uniform, with sister and mother behind. One of the disadvantages of an early holiday was the weather. John explains: 'It was quite early in the year and Easter can be quite cold. In those days also, there were no leisure clothes and one went away in one's everyday things. My mother appears to be wearing her fox fur over her shoulders. My brother is in full school uniform; he had nothing else to wear. By this time I had got my school certificate behind me and wished to disassociate myself from school outside school hours so would not have been wearing a school cap. I assure you that the coat is my own, but the trilby was borrowed for the photograph from my father.'
THE SPEIGHT FAMILY

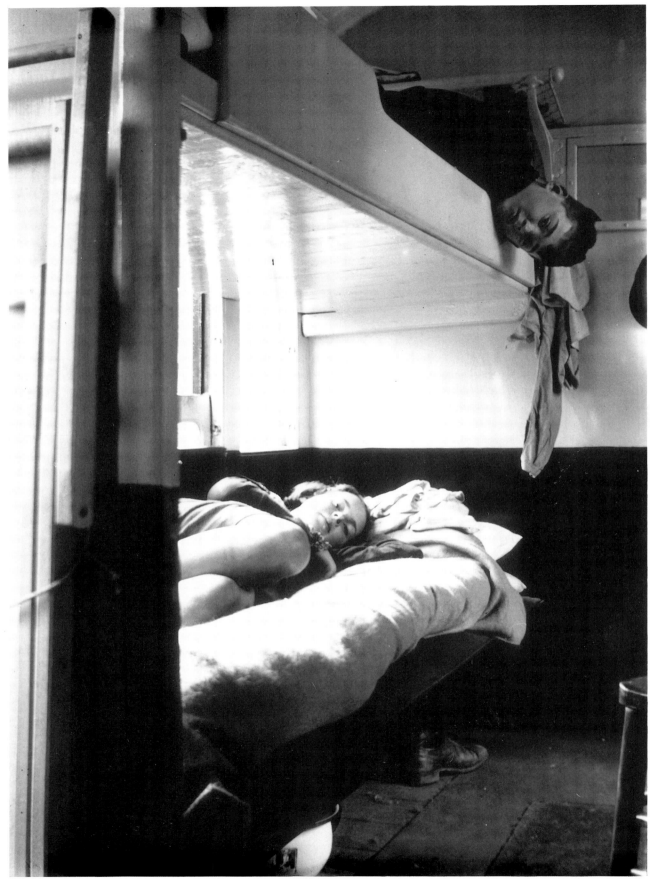

The compact interior of the children's bedroom complete with chamber pot under the bed.   THE SPEIGHT FAMILY

The view of the village from the camp coach window with the Valencia Hotel and Vicarage prominent on the bank of the river.
THE SPEIGHT FAMILY

Young Richard Speight with cloth cap drinking from the water container provided.
THE SPEIGHT FAMILY

A tranquil scene looking up towards the north end of the yard, showing the positioning of the camp coach. The coal wagons, including one from the Highley Mining Company, may have been awaiting repair.
THE SPEIGHT FAMILY

The village has changed little since 1938 although the footbridge has replaced the ferry and the castle has gone. The ferry was always a source of interest with the power of the current being employed to propel it. It was tethered to a pulley on a steel cable spanning the river. The pulley slipped along the cable in sharp irregular jerks as the ferry crossed to the other side.   THE SPEIGHT FAMILY

This view from the ferry shows the camp coach between the trees.   THE SPEIGHT FAMILY

THE SPEIGHT FAMILY

The ferry gliding gently across the river.

PASSENGERS CARRIED
AT OWN RISK

The Speight family holiday was taken up with walks and picnics in the area, both up and downstream and into the Wyre Forest. The upstream walk was to Hampton Loade, returning to Arley by train. On their walk downstream they saw the famous Victoria Bridge and the Elan Valley aqueduct. Top left: *Looking from the station to the village, with the castle on the skyline.* Top right: *Arley Castle, which at that time was used as a girls' school.* Right: *The island between Arley and Highley was a popular place for bathers.*
THE SPEIGHT FAMILY

With Victoria Bridge behind them, this picture was taken as the Speight family headed towards Trimpley, the Elan Valley aqueduct and Dowles Bridge.
THE SPEIGHT FAMILY

Picnic time by the side of the river.

Waiting for the train home. This holiday was never to be repeated as the camp coach was only based at Arley for one year — fond memories.
THE SPEIGHT FAMILY

Left: *LNER 0–6–0 No. 2141 on the 'down' platform at Arley, c.1945. Colin Dyson has the shunting pole.* Right: *Mrs. Jones and her grand-children outside the 'gents' in 1952. Allan and Jane are at the front with Mrs. Jones holding Elizabeth.*

GLADYS BILLINGHAM and CHRISTINE TURFORD

Left: *Porter/signalmen, Fred Jones and Jim Watson, in the small garden by the station entrance c.1952.* Right: *Mrs. Jones exchanging the token with her son, David, early in 1963, the last year of passenger operation. Note the morning newspapers attached to the token.*

GLADYS BILLINGHAM and BRIDGNORTH JOURNAL

The grandchildren again, selling pop and fruit from the station barrow in 1953. The cherries and plums were sold at 1/- a bag, the yellow plums being picked from the station yard.
CHRISTINE TURFORD

A large Prairie No. 8105 arriving at Arley on a local passenger train on 24th September 1955.   F. W. SHUTTLEWORTH

No. 6382 entering Arley station on 4th June 1960 on the 10.25 a.m. Hartlebury-Shrewsbury freight, with Fred Jones preparing to change tokens.
B. S. MOONE

No. 2251 heading a short up coal train through Arley c.1958.

PETER WARDLE

0—6—0 PT No. 3619 arriving at Arley on 29th September 1962.

R. J. SELLICK

An unidentified southbound railcar at Arley in 1954.

W. A. CAMWELL

W22W arriving at Arley on 14th July 1959.

MICHAEL HALE

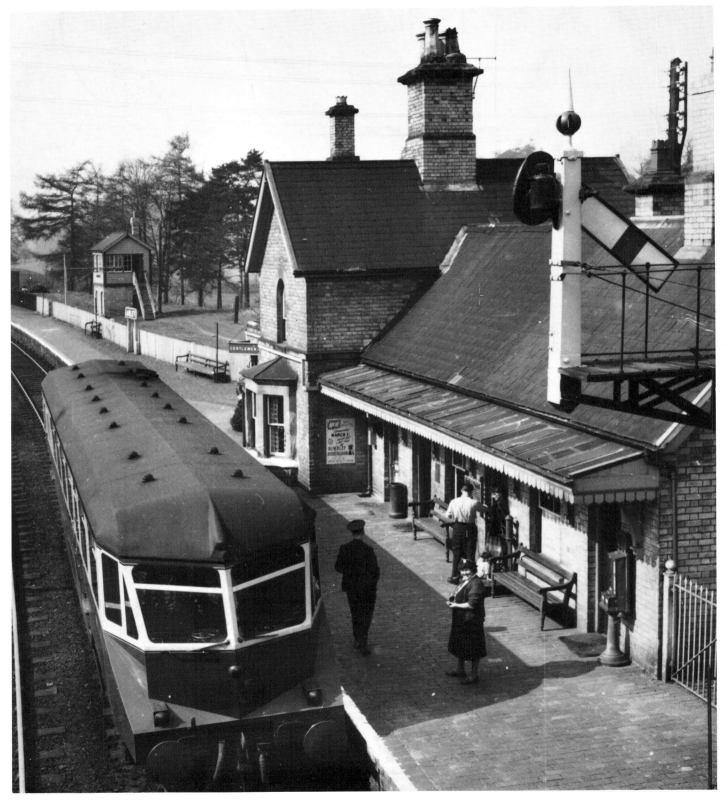

Railcar No. 19 on Good Friday, 16th April 1954, with a Hampton Loade-Bewdley workmen's special.
W. A. CAMWELL

Railcar No. 19 heading away south from Arley on 16th April 1954.

T. J. EDGINGTON

only months before closure, administrative control passed from the Western Region to the London Midland Region of British Railways and, despite objections, after 101 years of service, the last passenger train ran on 9th September and the last freight on 30th November. Details in the Clerk's Settlement Book show that the last entry was on 7th and 8th September 1963, when Fred Jones took:

£5	10	5	on trains
		6	on season tickets
	10	7	on excess fares
	2	0	on sundries
£6	3	6	Total debit

The Cloak Room Cash Book shows the last entry of 2s 6d for cycle storage (2 bikes at 1s 3d).

When Arley signal box was closed on 28th June 1964, Mrs. Jones moved to Bewdley and assisted in the station booking and parcels offices until its closure at the beginning of 1970 when she retired at the age of 68.

Mrs. Hall of the 'Harbour' recalls the day Fred died on 19th November 1970. He and Mrs. Jones had been poorly for some time. She had bought sufficient fish for both of them, cooked it at home and went down on the school bus with it. When their grandson met her he said, "Grandpa won't want this Mrs. Hall — he's dead." She went to see Mrs. Jones to commiserate with her and she told her that the kitchen clock had stopped at exactly the time Fred had died.

Continuing to live at Arley station, Mrs. Jones had been a familiar figure to all SVR volunteers engaged in restoration work at Arley in the early preservation days. It was indeed sad when she died on 15th January 1973 that she did not live to see the re-opening of the line which was something to which she was very much looking forward. A flowering cherry tree was planted in her memory in the newly established garden on the station's west platform by Colin May, the station master at that time, on Saturday, 18th February 1973.

Mrs. Jones as everyone remembers her.

GLADYS BILLINGHAM

The scene that greeted the first volunteers during the late summer of 1971. A formidable task lay ahead.

P. J. G. RANSOM

VOLUNTEER LABOURS

THAT any part of the Severn Valley Railway should be resurrected by a group of dedicated volunteers is a remarkable achievement by any standards, let alone the sixteen miles from Bridgnorth to Kidderminster. However, the line was opened in stages: from Bridgnorth to Hampton Loade on 23rd May 1970, to Highley on 12th April 1974, to Arley and Bewdley on 18th May 1974, and finally to Kidderminster on 30th July 1984. Each stage has its own story but by the time work began on Arley station, nature had a strong hold on the site.

As well as the weeds, the early days of restoration were beset with constant drainage problems and there was the added task of replacing the 'down' platform edge which had been demolished by British Railways because of clearance problems. Albert Jones, a retired ganger living in the village, regularly came to the station to help locate drains and pipe runs, even when well into his retirement. Albert, who was a real gentleman, used to work the length from Alveley to Victoria Bridge. It was a sad loss to the village and the station when he passed away on 13th October 1981, aged 87 years. Since 1971, Arley preservationists had their own regular band of senior citizens, including Andy Palmer, the late Tom McGhee, and George Lodge, who regularly attended and passed on their experience and knowledge to the younger generation. The general workforce changes year by year but the hard core remains, giving its all for the station.

The early restoration team was led by Colin May and Malcolm Broadhurst. Work continued at a rapid pace and in December 1974 the reinstatement of the 'up' main track was commenced. The work was undertaken by the then 'number 3' PW gang, assisted by members of the Arley station staff, and co-ordinated by Alun Rees, the chief engineer. Working south from the 'Highley end', the first task was to reinstate the north loop points, and fortunately the component

Malcolm Broadhurst and Colin May await the first train, but it is still three years away. The pile of bricks in the background was all that then remained of the old signal box.

B. S. MOONE

43

A year later and signs of an improvement with the station master at the time, Colin May, wheeling a barrow of cement across a plank during the platform wall rebuilding in September 1972.

AUTHOR

parts of the turnout had been left on site by BR. Some fifty yards further south, the siding points were then replaced in their previous position, using pointwork removed from the northern end of Eardington loop, which had been converted into a siding. The southern turnout from the Kinlet siding site was used as the connection between the two sidings. As the southern loop trackwork had been dismantled and some parts were missing altogether, it was decided to contract out the job of re-assembly to the Railway and General Engineering Co. at Nottingham, the switchplate, stock rails and crossing being the only items recoverable from Arley.

The first train to use the finished trackwork was a return evening 'special' on 17th May 1975, hauled by 46521.

The official re-opening of the station was performed on 18th May 1974. The station was declared 're-opened' at 11.45 a.m. precisely with the cutting of a tape strategically hung across the main entrance to the 'up' platform. This brief ceremony was kindly carried out by Lady Woodward,

The relaying gang reinstating the track under the guidance of Alun Rees with the 'Yorton' signal box taking shape in the background – Sunday, 26th January 1975.

B. S. MOONE

whose family associations with Arley probably date back at least as long as the railway itself. Both she and Mr. Richard Dunn, who introduced her, paid tribute to the volunteer labour force responsible for the restoration of the station. The guests then made their way to the waiting room for a cold buffet expertly prepared by Arley station's own restaurateur of the time, John Thomason, who also donated a number of bottles of wine and champagne to complement the barrel of 'Brew XI' presented by the Valentia Arms Hotel.

Musical accompaniment had meantime been provided by the eighteen members of the Cleobury Mortimer Silver Prize Band who, conducted by Ray Millichamp, reached a grand climax with the march 'Le Rêve Passe' as the day's first steam train, hauled by a resplendent 5764, edged its way slowly under the road bridge and into the station just before midday. The bell ringers of St. Peter's Church added their own welcome from the other side of the river, and a repeat performance was laid on for No. 43106 at the head of the first arrival from Bridgnorth, this time to the strains of 'Colonel Bogey'. To end a very successful first day, over a hundred fare-paying passengers began their journey from Arley.

Above: *Crowds flock in for the official re-opening of the station on 18th May 1974. Mr. Richard Dunn meets Lady Woodward (with white hat) on the platform.* B. S. MOONE

The Cleobury Mortimer Silver Prize Band providing the music while the first train, the 11.45 ex-Bewdley hauled by No. 5764, was awaiting departure.
JOHN HUNT

Passenger trains crossed at Arley on 25th May 1975, with No. 43106 on the 'up' crossing and No. 46521 on the 11.45 ex-Bewdley. The Bewdley North to Arley section was worked by the 'one engine in steam' train staff, whilst the Arley to Highley section was token operated, with the token instruments, as in BR and GWR days, situated in the station master's office. The signalman in charge on this first day was John Phillips, and hand signalmen were Alun Rees and John Garth.

The replacement signal box, which was rapidly taking shape at this time, had been located at Yorton (LNWR) near Shrewsbury. The all-wooden box was slightly larger than the original brick-based GWR one, regrettably demolished during early SVR days when it was felt impossible to ever purchase the southern section of line. The SVR Signals and Telegraph Dept. was able to use the remnants to aid the rebuilding of Bridgnorth signal box. The 'Yorton' box was stored at Eardington prior to erection at Arley. Construction

Repainting the up distant signal in March 1978. Men and equipment were transferred to site by pump trolley.   AUTHOR

No. 45110 entering Arley during the summer of 1974. Andrew Stephens is on platform duty.
B. S. MOONE

The station staff, August 1978. (Left to right) I. Truman; A. Smith; D. Evans, assistant station master; B. Geens, station master; M. Southall and P. Williams.   AUTHOR

of the box was continued over a number of years and credit is due to Alan Davies and his small team for a job well done. Originally the former Adderbury signal box was transferred to the SVR for re-use at Arley but was never used.

The first of the new signals, the down advanced starting and the up main home, were erected during March 1975. The up starting signal (ex-Llangollen) and down home bracket (ex-Bewdley viaduct) removed 4th January 1976, were erected later. The S and T Dept. installed the 30 lever frame salvaged from the Kidderminster station signal box and the restored box became operational with effect from Enthusiasts' Day on 10th April 1976, and token working between Arley and Bewdley North was completed in time for Easter 1976.

In the early 1970s, platform lamps were acquired from Bewdley and Selly Oak (Birmingham) stations, and more recently new square lamp tops of GWR style were purchased out of the station 'tea fund'. This has helped fund many projects and items of machinery and tools

No. 7812 Erlestoke Manor *on an 'up' passenger, passing No. 46521 on a works train, during the summer of 1982.*　　　MRS. R. J. GARRAD

The entrance to the main station buildings and 'up' platform.   AUTHOR

including the surfacing of the station car park in 1983. Money is raised through the station tea fund, food and drink being sold from the old weighbridge office which was given the name 'Syd's Cafe' in the early preservation days. Now completely rebuilt and extended, it has been renamed 'Tom's Cabin' in memory of Tom McGhee who had been the longest serving member of the station team until his death in 1989.

Tasks undertaken have included restoration of the station canopy, fence erection, general painting, and the development of large areas of garden which are now the pride of the station. Even the field, which adjoined the down platform gardens, has been drained and transformed into a two-acre picnic area. The planting of small trees and some landscaping now make the area very attractive and add to the station's appeal. Other demanding work has included rebuilding the main platform wall following frost damage. This kind of work is undertaken during the closed season in the early months of each year.

The main station buildings, looking towards Victoria Bridge and Bewdley in 1980.   DEREK MILLWARD

The interior of the station master's office, showing the ticket rack and counter. The hands of the clock are worked by a bar connected to the works in the pendulum box on the left. Another bar in turn operates the other clock face in the waiting room on the other side of the wall. The clock, which is owned by Gordon Allen, was originally from Newnham Bridge station. AUTHOR

My successor and current station master, Ian Latimer, now has to manage a huge commercial operation. The station is more popular now than at any time during its long history and carries more passengers in a Christmas weekend than in a whole year in pre-preservation days. During the Christmas running, when passengers are carried from Kidderminster to visit Father Christmas, a staff of up to fifty volunteers is mustered to ensure a smoothly-run operation. In addition to the train service, many other attractions are organised. The rail vehicles concerned are decorated inside and out and along with the carols and coloured lights, make a very impressive grotto. There are also musicians, choirs, Tom's Cabin sells hot mince pies and other hot refreshments, and, together with a variety of other stalls, a very seasonal atmosphere is created all round. All the staff, from the operating personnel to the refreshments team are really rushed off their feet, not to mention Father Christmas!

Time for a break during 'Santa' operations. Tom McGhee keeps the loco crew happy with some liquid refreshment.
BIRMINGHAM POST AND MAIL

Awarded commendations in previous years, the efforts of all concerned received recognition in 1983 when the station was awarded first prize in the National Best Restored Station competition organised by the Association of Railway Preservation Societies Ltd.

The restoration of the station has been due entirely to the team of volunteers spanning the years since 1971.

Sir Peter Parker, then Chairman of British Railways, who presented the Commendation Awards at Euston station, paid us a high compliment when he

DAVID WILCOCK

No. 46521 at Arley on 7th December 1980.

The rebuilt signal box. AUTHOR

These interior views show the two single line token instruments at the Highley end of the box. The train register desk and period style telephones are situated by the door at the station end. Two gas lamps provide interior lighting, supplied (together with the outside lamp) by bottled gas — no mains gas exists at the station. There is also an electric light. The nearest signal lever operates the down distant signal which, near Victoria Bridge, is 850 yards away and is battery operated. The up distant signal lever at the opposite end of the frame is 1,000 yards from the box and manually operated. As the wire route is far from straight this lever requires a little more effort to pull. The short lever in the centre is the switching out lever which is used when the signal box is not required. The token section then becomes Bewdley North to Highley. AUTHOR

The main station building and 'up' platform. The Ladies' room door on the right was added after 1910, replacing an existing window (see plans on pages 6 & 7). Access to the Ladies' waiting room and lavatory was formerly through the centre door which is now the station master's office. The booking office was then situated inside the general waiting room separated by a wooden partition which is still in use today and separates the porters room (left hand door, which also replaced a window) from the waiting room. The port-hole window in the house bedroom was added during preservation days.

AUTHOR'S COLLECTION

The inside view of the waiting room. The crush barrier was added in preservation days and came from Snow Hill station, Birmingham.
                                                                                    AUTHOR'S COLLECTION

visited the station on 30th July 1980. Under Ian Latimer, the station has continued to gain awards and commendations up to 1987 but has now been prevented from entering again for a while because of previous regular successes.

The station has continued to be a popular location for film companies. In my days at Arley, railway sequences for the films 'Candle Shoe' and 'The Thirty-nine Steps' were shot at the station and on Victoria Bridge. This brought stars like the late David Niven and Robert Powell to the station, 'The Thirty-nine Steps' was also my first as a film 'extra'. I was given the part of a policeman searching for Richard Hannay (Robert Powell). A popular TV series filmed on the railway was 'God's Wonderful Railway', the period depicting the war years being shot at Arley.

More recently, sequences for the films 'The Lost Empire', 'Hannay' and 'The Lion, the Witch and the Wardrobe' have been shot at Arley along with many other TV films and commercials.

Mr. Bob Reed, Chairman of British Rail, presenting the slate plaque to the author at the ceremony at Marylebone station on 28th February 1984.
                                                                    BRITISH RAILWAYS

The 1883-built waiting shelter on the 'down' platform. The land behind the shelter is now used as a picnic area which overlooks the station and village.
AUTHOR'S COLLECTION

The 1908 approach to the 'down' platform.

AUTHOR

The Arley station staff during the summer of 1991, with current station master, Ian Latimer.
AUTHOR'S COLLECTION

The uniform staff with station master Ian Latimer (on left). Ian has been station master since my departure in 1983 and has now completed over twelve years in this position.
AUTHOR'S COLLECTION

ARLEY FERRY

Table of Reduced Rates at which, for the present, persons may take out season tickets for periods of not less than three months, but only on pre-payment of the amount charged.

							Per Quarter
One person	At the rate of	...	...	3/3
Two persons (of the same household)	,,	,,	...	...	4/4
Three ,,	,,	,,	,,	,,	...	...	5/5
Four ,,	,,	,,	,,	,,	...	...	6/6
Five ,,	,,	,,	,,	,,	...	...	8/1½
Six ,,	,,	,,	,,	...	...	9/9
Seven ,,	,,	,,	,,	,,	...	...	11/4½
Eight ,,	,,	,,	,,	,,	...	...	13/-

The above concessions from the ordinary full ferry tolls payable being entirely voluntary on the part of the owner of the Ferry may be modified or withdrawn altogether at any time.

April, 1887.

THE VILLAGE

Today Arley station is connected to the village by means of a footbridge over the river, but before this, for some six centuries, a ferry plied to and fro between the north and south banks of the Severn. First mention of the ferry was in the Close Rolls for 1323-7, but it was not until 1602 that a regular service commenced. As well as conveying passengers, the ferry used to carry wagons, carts, horses and general livestock. In 1931 the ferry journey cost one penny per person, except for children going to school and people going to church who were carried free. The ferry closed in 1972 and was replaced by the footbridge which was built at a cost of £43,500.

This interesting photograph, taken in 1907, shows the ferry with various modes of transport which regularly used the crossing.

Courtesy PROF. L. J. WILLS

Sunset at Arley c.1948. The picture also shows the location of the Cider House on the opposite bank of the river. Arley must have been a very different place for there used to be no fewer than six inns within a short distance of each other. There was the 'Valentia' with its skittle alley in what is now the vicarage garden, the 'Crown' in what is now the 'Valentia' car park, the scene of many a cock fight and pony race, the 'Cock' which was situated on the river bank near the vicarage garden, the 'Nelson' which occupied the site of the new Post Office and Stores, and of course the 'Harbour' which is still in business close to the station.

AUTHOR'S COLLECTION

Arley was the most northerly of the Severn ferries in Worcestershire and the last to survive. Bert Evans, a native of Upper Arley, worked the ferry for 32 years until closure on 22nd January 1972. His expert handling of the 38-ton boat won him the Royal Humane Society award in 1957 when he rescued a runaway ferry which had broken its moorings at Hampton Loade further up the river. At one time the Severn Valley Railway had hoped to purchase the ferry and run it as a summer tourist attraction. This, alas, was not to be, and the ferry is now (1985) moored alongside the North Quay at Bewdley.   Courtesy BERT EVANS

Arley has a long history and traces of Roman camps could still be seen in the area until recent times, no doubt proving that some of the British-Roman battles were fought in the area. The first mention of Arley occurs in 996 AD during the reign of Ethelred 'the Unready'. Arley is also mentioned in the Domesday Book of 1085-86 during the reign of William the Conqueror. The overall appearance of the village has changed little during the past 100 years with the exception of the footbridge and the demise of the Castle. The 'Cock' Inn on the extreme left of this view and the Cider House mentioned earlier were demolished in the 1960s.
                                                                                    AUTHOR'S COLLECTION

The new Post Office and Stores on the right still enjoys a brisk business today but the buildings on the left have since been demolished.
                                                                        Courtesy GEORGE BLOUNT

The landing stage and Valentia Hotel c.1900.   FRITH, courtesy WORCESTER COUNTY RECORDS OFFICE

The Valentia Hotel, c.1910.   FRITH, courtesy WORCESTER COUNTY RECORDS OFFICE

The Vicarage and Tower c.1910. The Tower was built around 1800 by the Lord of the Manor, Lord Mountnorris, in the same style as the Castle.
AUTHOR'S COLLECTION

The village street c.1910 from near the church, looking towards the Tower. Tom Price, with straw hat, is standing outside the old cottages in the doorway of what was part of the butcher's shop. New bungalows were built in their place during 1964-65.
AUTHOR'S COLLECTION

The present church was built by Henry de Port in 1135. Built of rose coloured limestone, it has now been much restored, although it still retains a great deal of its antiquity. Portions of Norman work from an earlier building are still to be seen in the present fabric. It consisted of a nave and chancel, but the south wall of the nave is all that now remains of the 12th century building. The north aisle was added around 1325 when the chancel arch was also rebuilt in its present form. In 1400 a tower was built at the west end of the nave. Early in the 16th century the walls of the nave were raised by the addition of a clerestory, and later that century the tower was built on foundations which can still be seen of the earlier one. The present chancel, with the vestry and organ chamber, was built in 1885. At the same time the old pews were removed, the floor lowered, and seats made from oak felled in the parish were installed. The church was closed for fourteen months during the restoration and Hexton's Quarry provided the new stone required. During this time the Sunday services were held in the great dining room of the Castle, set apart temporarily for this purpose. The peal of six bells drifting up the valley over the waters of the Severn is a pleasure not easily forgotten.

AUTHOR'S COLLECTION

Church, Arley

Arley Church

AUTHOR'S COLLECTION

It was during the time of George, 2nd Earl of Mountnorris, born at the Manor House of Arley in December 1770, that great changes took place at the Manor which had been known hitherto as Areley Hall. All the kitchens and servants' quarters of the house, and the stables adjoining, were pulled down and rebuilt as a modern castle, or 'folly', but the Earl died in 1844 before the work was complete, and the remaining alterations were not carried out. The Castle, a popular landmark at Arley for over a hundred years, had in more recent years been let as a girls' school. The school had over sixty 12-18 year old boarders plus staff, many of whom came by train. Their luggage came in huge trunks trundled down the hill from the station, over the river on the ferry, and up to the Castle. The Lord of the Manor found the cost of maintaining the Castle increasingly great and in 1959, after some neglect, the Castle and Manor including 700 acres of the Estate, changed hands. The new owner had the Castle demolished between 5th February 1962 and 19th July 1963 and the only part of any significance remaining today is the Barbican Tower. It has been said that a mansion has stood on the site of the Arley Castle since Norman days when it was customary to build on, or have within the courtyard, a spring of water, which of course proved invaluable in cases of siege. Such a spring was to be found underneath the drawing room floor of the Castle.

Some of the older inhabitants, who remember the Castle with affection, were very sad to see it go. To them it was really beautiful; as one elderly villager remarked, "No matter where you went, you could always see the Castle — along the road from Trimpley, along the road from Shatterford — it stood out, it was really something." AUTHOR'S COLLECTION

The fine ornate surround of the library fireplace in the Castle, 1958.
NATIONAL MONUMENTS RECORD